STUDY

"But in your hearts revere Christ as Lord. Always be prepared to give an answer to everyone who asks you to give the reason for the hope that you have. But do this with gentleness and respect" **1 Peter 3:15 (NIV)**

Before You Begin: Proof of the Bible's Authenticity	1
Introduction to the Study	6
Session 1: Seeking God	9
Session 2: The Word of God	15
Session 3: Discipleship	20
Session 4: Coming of the Kingdom	25
Session 5: Light and Darkness	30
Session 6: New Testament Conversion	35
Session 7: The Cross	42
Session 8: Baptism with the Holy Spirit	48
Session 9: Miraculous Gifts of the Holy Spirit	54
Session 10: The Church	61
Session 11: Acts 1 - 28	66
Session 12: After Baptism, Now What	72
Session 13: Christ is Your Life	78
Session 14: Building Strong Spiritual Relationships	84
Session 15: The Mission	90
Session 16: Persecution	96
Your Life, Your Baptism, Your Calling	101

BEFORE YOU BEGIN: PROOF OF THE BIBLE'S AUTHENTICITY & DIVINE INSPIRATION

The Bible is an unparalleled compilation of 66 books authored by approximately 40 different individuals over 1,500 years. This extraordinary composition stands alone in human history, highlighting its unique nature and warranting serious consideration as a significant text. While the mere fact of its complex authorship does not automatically prove it to be the word of God, it sets the stage for deeper exploration of its divine inspiration.

Archaeological Evidence Supporting the Bible

Archaeological discoveries have indeed provided substantial support for the historical accuracy of the Bible, both in the Old and New Testaments. Findings continue to affirm that the people, places, and events described in Scripture were real and accurately recorded.

- **The Hittite Empire** – Once thought to be a myth, this civilization was confirmed through archaeological excavations that revealed its existence, validating the Bible's references to the Hittites (Blue Letter Bible).

- **The Tel Dan Inscription (1993)** – This discovery provided the first extra-biblical evidence of King David, with an Aramaic inscription referring to the "House of David" (Biblical Archaeology Society, Christian Research Institute).

- **The Pilate Stone (1961)** – A stone inscription confirming the existence of Pontius Pilate, the Roman prefect who presided over the trial of Jesus, corroborating the biblical account (Bible Archaeology Report).

- **The Dead Sea Scrolls (1947-1956)** – These ancient manuscripts, dating back over 2,000 years, include Old Testament texts that confirm the remarkable consistency of Scripture over time, proving the accuracy and preservation of biblical prophecy and teachings.

These examples demonstrate how archaeological findings have consistently reinforced the Bible's reliability as a historical document, underscoring that the events and figures mentioned in its texts were real and accurately recorded by those who witnessed them.

Scientific Evidence Supporting Jesus' Existence

While faith in Christ does not require scientific validation, many historians and scientists acknowledge that Jesus of Nazareth was a real historical figure. The **vast majority of scholars—both religious and secular—agree that Jesus lived and was crucified under Pontius Pilate.**

- Dr. Bart Ehrman, a leading secular historian and former skeptic, has stated, *"The idea that Jesus never existed is a myth; virtually every historian agrees that He was a real historical figure."*

- Renowned physicist Dr. Frank Tipler, in his book *The Physics of Christianity*, argues that **scientific**

principles align with Christian theology, further reinforcing the credibility of biblical claims.

- A study published in the *Journal for the Study of the Historical Jesus* analyzed the extensive historical documentation supporting Jesus, concluding that the evidence for His life and death is stronger than for many ancient historical figures.

The Bible's Prophetic Accuracy

The Bible's prophetic nature sets it apart from any other religious text. The Old Testament contains over 300 prophecies detailing the coming of the Messiah. Remarkably, these prophecies were fulfilled with astonishing precision by Jesus Christ:

- **Born in Bethlehem** – As foretold in Micah 5:2.
- **Betrayed for 30 pieces of silver** – As predicted in Zechariah 11:12-13.
- **Crucified (before crucifixion was invented)** – As prophesied in Psalm 22:16.

Critics may argue that these prophecies were written or modified post-event to align with Jesus' life. However, the existence of the **Septuagint**, a Greek translation of the Old Testament completed around 250 B.C., precludes this possibility. This ancient document demonstrates that these prophecies were indeed recorded centuries before Jesus' birth, affirming the Bible's prophetic accuracy and divine foresight.

Scripture itself reinforces the divine origin of prophecy:

- **2 Peter 1:21** – "For prophecy never had its origin in the human will, but prophets, though human, spoke from God as they were carried along by the Holy Spirit."

- **2 Timothy 3:16** – "All Scripture is God-breathed and is useful for teaching, rebuking, correcting and training in righteousness."

These passages underscore the belief that the Bible is inspired by God and carries His authoritative message.

Statistical Impossibility of Jesus' Fulfillment of Prophecy

One of the most compelling pieces of evidence is Jesus' fulfillment of over **300 Old Testament messianic prophecies**. The probability of a single individual fulfilling just eight of these prophecies is staggering—**one in 10^{17} (1 followed by 17 zeros)**. To visualize this, if you filled the state of Texas two feet deep with coins and marked just one coin, the chance of someone picking the marked coin on their first try is the same as fulfilling eight prophecies.

The probability of fulfilling **48 prophecies** increases exponentially to **one in 10^{157}**, which is akin to lining up electrons and taking 19 million years to count them all. **This makes it statistically impossible for anyone to fulfill these prophecies by chance—yet Jesus fulfilled over 300 of them.**

(Peter Stoner's Calculations in his book, Science Speaks, backed by H. Harold Hartzler, PhD, of the American Scientific Affiliation, Goshen College.)

Conclusion: The Bible's Divine Inspiration and Jesus' Authenticity

The Bible's unparalleled composition, confirmed historical accuracy, fulfillment of detailed prophecies, and scientific affirmation of Jesus' existence present a compelling case for its divine inspiration. These factors collectively provide a robust foundation for believing that the Bible is indeed the Word of God, worthy of deep respect and earnest study.

Jesus Christ is not just a religious figure—His life, death, and resurrection are backed by history, archaeology, and prophecy. The overwhelming body of evidence, from ancient manuscripts to statistical probabilities, makes it clear that faith in Christ is not blind faith, but faith rooted in **truth, history, and divine revelation.**

KNOW THE TRUTH

A Foundational Study for Baptism Preparation

Welcome to *Know the Truth: A Foundational Study for Baptism Preparation*. If you're reading this, it means you're curious about faith, God, and what it means to follow Jesus. Maybe you're searching for answers, trying to understand your purpose, or simply wanting to learn more about who Jesus is. Wherever you are on your journey, you are in the right place.

This study is designed to help you explore the foundational truths of Christianity. You don't need to have it all figured out. In fact, this is a space for you to ask questions, reflect, and discover what faith in Jesus truly means. This study provides the knowledge and understanding you need to make an informed choice about your faith.

Why Is a Strong Foundation Important?

Let's think about building a house. If the foundation isn't solid, the house can't stand strong when storms come. Life is like that too. We all face challenges, doubts, and struggles. Having a strong foundation helps you navigate those storms with hope and purpose.

Jesus shared this story in Matthew 7:24-25:

"Therefore everyone who hears these words of mine and puts them into practice is like a wise man who built his house on the rock. The rain came down, the streams rose, and the winds blew and beat against that house; yet it did not fall, because it had its foundation on the rock."

This study will help you explore what it means to build your life on a solid foundation—the truth about who God is and who you are.

Understanding the Battle We Face

As you learn more about faith, you'll discover that there's a spiritual reality we often overlook. The Bible tells us there's an enemy who wants to keep us from knowing the truth and experiencing the life God created us for. But here's the good news: God has provided everything we need to stand strong and find true freedom.

In Ephesians 6:10-11, the Bible says:

"Finally, be strong in the Lord and in His mighty power. Put on the full armor of God so that you can take your stand against the devil's schemes."

What Is the Armor of God?

The armor of God isn't physical armor—it's spiritual armor. It's about being prepared to face life's challenges with strength and courage:

- **The Belt of Truth:** Knowing what's true helps you stand firm when life feels confusing.

- **The Breastplate of Righteousness:** When you choose to live rightly, your heart is protected.

- **The Gospel of Peace:** Understanding God's love brings peace, even when life is hard.

- **The Shield of Faith:** Faith helps you trust in what you can't see, especially when doubts arise.

- **The Helmet of Salvation:** Knowing you're valued and loved by God protects your mind from negativity.

- **The Sword of the Spirit:** This is the Bible—God's Word that guides, strengthens, and protects us.

Prayer is like your lifeline, connecting you to God anytime, anywhere. Ephesians 6:18

"And pray in the Spirit on all occasions with all kinds of prayers and requests."

What You'll Learn in This Study

This study will guide you through the basics of the Christian faith:

- Who is God, and why does He matter?
- What is the Bible, and how can it help you?
- Who is Jesus, and what did He do for us?
- What does it mean to follow Jesus?
- Why is baptism important?
- How do you grow in faith, even when life gets hard?

You don't have to believe everything right away. This is a journey—a chance to explore, ask questions, and discover the truth for yourself. As you go through each session, you'll learn about God's love, the purpose He has for your life, and how to find hope, peace, and direction.

We're glad you're here. Let's take this journey together.

SESSION ONE:
SEEKING GOD

Discovering the Heart of God Through Pursuit

Seeking God is the first and most essential step in any spiritual journey. Before we understand baptism, salvation, or discipleship, we must first understand the heart of the One we are seeking. God desires to be known—not just as a distant Creator, but as a personal Father, Savior, and Lord.

God's Word assures us that when we seek Him with sincerity, He will reveal Himself to us. This study will help us explore the importance of seeking God, how He calls us into a deeper relationship, and the blessings that come from wholeheartedly pursuing Him.

Key Scripture: Jeremiah 29:11-13

"For I know the plans I have for you," declares the Lord, "plans to prosper you and not to harm you, plans to give you hope and a future. Then you will call on me and come and pray to me, and I will listen to you. You will seek me and find me when you seek me with all your heart."

God's promise in Jeremiah 29 reveals that He has a divine plan for each of us, one filled with hope and a future. However, this promise is tied to our pursuit of Him. He assures us that when we call on Him, pray, and seek Him with all our hearts, He will respond.

But what does it truly mean to seek God with all our hearts? It means placing Him at the center of our lives, prioritizing Him above all else, and earnestly desiring His presence in every aspect of our journey.

The Example of Jesus: Seeking God's Will Through Prayer and Obedience

One of the most powerful examples of seeking God is found in the life of Jesus. Before starting His public ministry, Jesus sought God through prayer and fasting. In Matthew 4:1-11, He spent forty days in the wilderness, resisting temptation and fully surrendering to God's will. His life was marked by continual communion with the Father, demonstrating that seeking God is an ongoing journey, not just a one-time event.

Lessons from Jesus' Example:

- **Prayer as a Priority:** Jesus regularly withdrew to pray (Luke 5:16), showing that seeking God requires intentional time in His presence.

- **Obedience to God's Will:** Jesus followed God's direction even when it was difficult, teaching us that true seeking leads to surrender.

- **Relying on Scripture:** When tempted, Jesus responded with God's Word (Matthew 4:4), emphasizing that knowing Scripture helps us stay close to God.

- **Dependence on the Holy Spirit:** Jesus was led by the Spirit into the wilderness (Luke 4:1), showing that seeking God involves spiritual reliance.

Why Seeking God Matters

1. God's Plans Unfold as We Seek Him

Seeking God is not about earning His love—He already loves us fully. It's about aligning ourselves with His will. As we pursue Him, He reveals His plans, opens doors, and provides wisdom.

God often calls us to trust Him before He reveals the next step. Proverbs 3:5-6 encourages us to rely on Him rather than our own understanding, promising that He will make our paths straight.

2. Seeking God Leads to Spiritual Growth

Just as a plant grows when watered, our faith grows when we spend time in God's presence. Reading Scripture, praying, and surrounding ourselves with other believers strengthen our faith and understanding.

- **Faith Deepens:** As we seek God, our understanding of His character grows, leading to greater trust in Him.

- **Spiritual Discernment Develops:** Seeking God sharpens our ability to recognize His voice and direction.

- **Transformation Occurs:** Our thoughts, attitudes, and actions become more aligned with Christ.

3. Seeking God Brings Peace and Direction

Life is full of uncertainties, but those who seek God find clarity and peace.

- **Overcoming Anxiety:** Philippians 4:6-7 reminds us to bring our worries to God through prayer, promising His peace in return.

- **Finding Purpose:** Seeking God helps us discover His specific calling for our lives.

- **Building Confidence:** When we know we are walking in God's will, we can face challenges with courage.

Barriers to Seeking God

Many things can hinder our pursuit of God. Identifying and removing these obstacles is crucial for a thriving relationship with Him.

1. **Distractions:** Busy schedules, social media, and entertainment can take priority over God.

2. **Sin and Unrepentance:** Sin creates a barrier between us and God. Confession and repentance restore our connection.

3. **Lack of Desire:** Sometimes, we become spiritually complacent. Asking God to renew our hunger for Him can reignite our pursuit.

4. **Fear of Surrender:** Seeking God fully means yielding control. Trusting His plans over our own can be challenging but rewarding.

Practical Ways to Seek God Daily

1. **Daily Prayer:** Start and end your day with intentional time talking to God.

2. **Bible Study:** Read God's Word daily, allowing it to shape your heart and mind.
3. **Worship and Praise:** Spend time in worship through music and thanksgiving.
4. **Fellowship with Other Believers:** Join a Bible study or church community for encouragement.
5. **Journaling:** Write down prayers, reflections, and insights from your spiritual journey.
6. **Fasting:** Setting aside distractions to focus on God can deepen our relationship with Him.
7. **Serving Others:** Seeking God is not just personal—it involves loving and serving others as Christ did.

Reflection Questions

1. What are some distractions that keep me from seeking God fully?
2. How can I be more intentional about spending time with God each day?
3. In what ways do I feel God calling me to deepen my relationship with Him?
4. How has seeking God changed my perspective on life's challenges?
5. What is one step I can take today to seek God more earnestly?

Disciple's Prayer

"Lord, You have invited me to seek You with all my heart, and You have promised that when I do, I will find You. Remove the distractions that keep me from pursuing You wholeheartedly. Align my heart with Yours, and reveal Your will and purpose for my life. I want to know You, trust You, and follow You—every step of the way. In Jesus' name, Amen."

Seeking God is the foundation of true discipleship. Before we follow Jesus into the waters of baptism, we must first follow Him into a life of seeking God with all our hearts. This pursuit is not about rules or religion—it is about relationship.

As we continue in this study, may our hearts be open to discovering more of God's truth, His love, and His perfect plan for our lives. Let us commit to seeking Him daily, trusting that He will guide us into His purpose and transform our hearts as we grow in faith.

SESSION TWO:
THE WORD OF GOD

Building Your Life on God's Truth Introduction

The Bible is more than a collection of ancient writings—it is the living Word of God, the foundation of our faith, and the ultimate source of truth for our lives. Before and after baptism, the Word of God plays a vital role in shaping us into disciples of Jesus. Every decision we make, every belief we hold, and every step we take should be informed and guided by Scripture.

Understanding God's Word is essential for knowing His will, growing in faith, and staying grounded in truth. In this session, we will explore why God's Word is necessary for every disciple, how it anchors us in truth, and how we can apply it in our daily lives.

Key Scriptures
2 Timothy 3:16-17
"All Scripture is God-breathed and is useful for teaching, rebuking, correcting and training in righteousness, so that the servant of God may be thoroughly equipped for every good work."

Hebrews 4:12
"For the word of God is alive and active. Sharper than any double-edged sword, it penetrates even to dividing soul and spirit, joints and marrow; it judges the thoughts and attitudes of the heart."

Romans 10:17
"Consequently, faith comes from hearing the message, and the message is heard through the word about Christ."

God's Word is not just a book of history or religious doctrine—it is **alive and active**, meaning it speaks to us today, convicts us, and transforms us. Without it, we would be spiritually lost, unsure of what is right and wrong, and unable to grow in our walk with Christ.

The Power of God's Word

1. Scripture Reveals God's Truth

We live in a world where truth is often subjective, shaped by culture, personal experiences, or emotions. But God's Word provides an **absolute standard** of truth that does not change. It exposes lies and helps us distinguish between right and wrong.

- **John 17:17** – *"Sanctify them by the truth; your word is truth."*
- **Psalm 119:105** – *"Your word is a lamp for my feet, a light on my path."*

The Bible teaches us how to live according to God's ways and **guides us in the right direction**.

2. The Word of God Transforms Our Lives

When we read and apply God's Word, it changes us from the inside out. The Bible **renews our minds** and helps us become more like Christ.

- **Romans 12:2** – *"Do not conform to the pattern of this world, but be transformed by the renewing of your mind. Then you will be able to test and approve what God's will is—his good, pleasing and perfect will."*
- **James 1:22** – *"Do not merely listen to the word, and so deceive yourselves. Do what it says."*

God's Word is not just something to read—it is something to **obey**. The more we apply it, the more it shapes our character, attitudes, and decisions.

3. The Bible Equips Us for Every Good Work
Scripture is a tool that prepares us for the challenges and responsibilities of discipleship. It corrects us when we go astray, strengthens us in times of difficulty, and empowers us to do God's work.

- **2 Timothy 3:16-17** teaches that all Scripture is **useful for teaching, correcting, and training** in righteousness.

- **Ephesians 6:17** calls the Word of God the **"sword of the Spirit"**, meaning it is a powerful weapon in our spiritual battles.

If we want to be **effective disciples of Jesus**, we must know and use the Word of God daily.

How to Build Your Life on God's Word

1. Daily Bible Reading
Just as we need daily food for our bodies, we need daily Scripture for our souls. Make a habit of reading the Bible every day, even if it's just a few verses. Start with the Gospels, Psalms, or Proverbs to develop a routine.

2. Studying the Bible in Depth
Reading is good, but studying brings deeper understanding. Use tools like commentaries, study guides, and Bible dictionaries to dig into the meaning of the text. Ask yourself:

- What is the context of this passage?
- What does this reveal about God's character?
- How does this apply to my life today?

3. Memorizing Scripture
When we memorize God's Word, we store His truth in our hearts, making it easier to recall in difficult moments.

- **Psalm 119:11** – *"I have hidden your word in my heart that I might not sin against you."*
- **Joshua 1:8** – *"Keep this Book of the Law always on your lips; meditate on it day and night, so that you may be careful to do everything written in it."*

4. Applying the Word in Your Life
The Bible is meant to be **lived out**, not just studied. Ask the Holy Spirit to help you put what you read into practice. Each day, seek to:
- Love others as Christ loves (John 13:34-35)
- Forgive as Christ forgave you (Colossians 3:13)
- Trust God in all circumstances (Proverbs 3:5-6)

5. Teaching and Sharing God's Word
One of the best ways to learn Scripture is to **share it with others**. Teach a Bible study, share verses with friends, or encourage others with Scripture in times of need.

Reflection Questions

1. How has reading God's Word shaped your understanding of baptism and discipleship?
2. What challenges do you face in making Scripture a daily part of your life?
3. In what areas of your life do you need to apply God's Word more intentionally?
4. How can you encourage others to build their lives on God's Word?

Disciple's Prayer

"Lord, Your Word is a lamp to my feet and a light to my path. Help me to treasure it, study it, and apply it daily. Shape my thoughts and actions through Your truth. Teach me to walk in obedience, trusting that Your Word will guide me in every season of life. Thank You for speaking through Scripture and drawing me closer to You. In Jesus' name, Amen."

God's Word is the foundation of faith and discipleship. It equips us, transforms us, and leads us closer to Christ. As we continue in this study, let us commit to knowing, loving, and obeying the Bible, building our lives on the truth that never changes.

SESSION THREE:
DISCIPLESHIP

Walking in the Footsteps of Jesus

Discipleship is more than just believing in Jesus—it is about following Him wholeheartedly. Throughout the Gospels, Jesus did not merely invite people to acknowledge Him as the Son of God; He called them to leave their old lives behind and walk in His footsteps. This commitment to discipleship is central to understanding baptism and what it means to live as a Christian.

Baptism is not an end but a beginning. It is the starting point of a transformed life where we commit to learning from Jesus, growing in our faith, and making more disciples. In this session, we will explore what it means to be a disciple, the cost of discipleship, and the responsibilities that come with following Jesus.

Key Scriptures

Mark 1:17
"Come, follow me," Jesus said, "and I will send you out to fish for people."

Luke 9:23-24
"Then he said to them all: 'Whoever wants to be my disciple must deny themselves and take up their cross daily and follow me. For whoever wants to save their life will lose it, but whoever loses their life for me will save it.'"

Matthew 28:19-20

"Therefore go and make disciples of all nations, baptizing them in the name of the Father and of the Son and of the Holy Spirit, and

teaching them to obey everything I have commanded you. And surely I am with you always, to the very end of the age."

Jesus' call to discipleship is not just for a select few—it is for all who choose to follow Him. His Great Commission commands us not only to be disciples but to make disciples, spreading the good news and guiding others in their faith journey.

What It Means to Be a Disciple

1. A Disciple is a Follower of Jesus

The word "disciple" means "learner" or "follower." Being a disciple of Jesus means committing to His teachings and walking in His ways. It is a lifelong journey of growing in faith and obedience.

- **John 8:31-32** – *"If you hold to my teaching, you are really my disciples. Then you will know the truth, and the truth will set you free."*

- **1 John 2:6** – *"Whoever claims to live in him must live as Jesus did."*

2. A Disciple Denies Themselves and Takes Up Their Cross

Discipleship is not about personal comfort or convenience. Jesus made it clear that following Him requires self-denial and total surrender to God's will.

- **Matthew 16:24-25** – *"Whoever wants to be my disciple must deny themselves and take up their cross and follow me."*

- **Philippians 3:8** – *"I consider everything a loss because of the surpassing worth of knowing Christ Jesus my Lord, for whose sake I have lost all things."*

3. A Disciple is Transformed by the Holy Spirit

Becoming a disciple is not just about modifying behavior; it is about experiencing a transformation of heart and mind through the Holy Spirit.

- **Romans 12:2** – *"Do not conform to the pattern of this world, but be transformed by the renewing of your mind."*

- **Galatians 5:22-23** – *"But the fruit of the Spirit is love, joy, peace, forbearance, kindness, goodness, faithfulness, gentleness and self-control."*

The Cost of Discipleship

Jesus never promised an easy path for His followers. He warned that discipleship requires sacrifice, but He also assured that the reward is far greater than the cost.

1. Leaving the Old Life Behind

- **Luke 14:33** – *"In the same way, those of you who do not give up everything you have cannot be my disciples."*

- **2 Corinthians 5:17** – *"Therefore, if anyone is in Christ, the new creation has come: The old has gone, the new is here!"*

2. **Facing Challenges and Persecution**

- **John 15:18-19** – *"If the world hates you, keep in mind that it hated me first."*

- **2 Timothy 3:12** – *"In fact, everyone who wants to live a godly life in Christ Jesus will be persecuted."*

Making Disciples

The call to discipleship is not just about personal growth—it is about multiplication. Jesus calls every disciple to make more disciples.

1. Teaching Others the Word of God

- **Matthew 28:20** – *"Teaching them to obey everything I have commanded you."*

- **2 Timothy 2:2** – *"And the things you have heard me say in the presence of many witnesses entrust to reliable people who will also be qualified to teach others."*

2. Living as a Witness for Christ

- **Acts 1:8** – *"You will receive power when the Holy Spirit comes on you; and you will be my witnesses."*

- **1 Peter 3:15** – *"Always be prepared to give an answer to everyone who asks you to give the reason for the hope that you have."*

Practical Applications

1. **Daily Commitment** – Spend time in prayer, Bible study, and worship to grow in your walk with Christ.

2. **Serving Others** – Look for opportunities to live out your faith by serving and loving others as Jesus did.

3. **Accountability & Fellowship** – Surround yourself with fellow believers who will encourage and challenge you in your faith.

4. **Sharing Your Faith** – Be intentional in telling others about Jesus and helping them begin their discipleship journey.

Reflection Questions

1. In what areas of your life do you need to fully surrender to Jesus?
2. How can you be more intentional in growing as a disciple of Christ?
3. Who in your life can you disciple and help grow in their faith?
4. What sacrifices are you willing to make to follow Jesus more closely?

Disciple's Prayer

"Lord, I surrender my life to You. Teach me to follow You wholeheartedly, to deny myself, and to take up my cross daily. Transform my heart and mind so that I may walk in Your ways. Give me the courage to share Your truth and make disciples for Your Kingdom. Strengthen me through Your Spirit and help me remain faithful in all circumstances. In Jesus' name, Amen."

Discipleship is a lifelong journey of walking with Jesus, learning from Him, and helping others do the same. As we continue this study, let us embrace the call to follow Christ with all our hearts, trusting that He will guide and empower us every step of the way.

SESSION FOUR:
COMING OF THE KINGDOM

Living Under the Rule of Christ

The Kingdom of God is central to Jesus' message and mission. From the beginning of His ministry, He proclaimed that the Kingdom had arrived, calling people to repent and believe the good news. But what does this Kingdom mean for us today? How does it relate to baptism? And how do we live as Kingdom citizens?

Understanding baptism requires understanding God's Kingdom. Baptism is not just a symbolic ritual—it is the defining moment when we step into the rule and reign of Jesus. It marks our transfer from the domain of darkness into the Kingdom of God's beloved Son (Colossians 1:13). This session will explore the arrival of God's Kingdom, the role of baptism in entering it, and what it means to live as a disciple under Christ's rule.

Key Scriptures

Matthew 3:1-2
"In those days John the Baptist came, preaching in the wilderness of Judea and saying, 'Repent, for the kingdom of heaven has come near.'"

Colossians 1:13-14
"For he has rescued us from the dominion of darkness and brought us into the kingdom of the Son he loves, in whom we have redemption, the forgiveness of sins."

Matthew 6:9-10
"This, then, is how you should pray: 'Our Father in heaven,

hallowed be your name, your kingdom come, your will be done, on earth as it is in heaven.'"

The Kingdom of God is not just a future promise; it is a present reality that began with Jesus and continues through His followers. To be baptized is to declare our allegiance to Christ's Kingdom and commit to living under His rule.

The Arrival of the Kingdom

1. Jesus Proclaimed the Kingdom

Jesus' ministry began with the announcement of God's Kingdom. He preached that the reign of God was at hand and called people to repentance and faith.

- **Mark 1:15** – *"The time has come," he said. "The kingdom of God has come near. Repent and believe the good news!"*

- **Luke 4:43** – *"But he said, 'I must proclaim the good news of the kingdom of God to the other towns also, because that is why I was sent.'"*

Jesus' message was clear: God's rule was breaking into the world, and people needed to respond by turning away from sin and following Him.

2. Baptism as Entry into the Kingdom

Baptism is the defining moment when we move from the world's kingdom to God's Kingdom. It is not just about forgiveness—it is about transformation and new citizenship.

- **John 3:5** – *"Jesus answered, 'Very truly I tell you, no one can enter the kingdom of God unless they are born of water and the Spirit.'"*

- **Acts 2:38** – *"Peter replied, 'Repent and be baptized, every one of you, in the name of Jesus Christ for the forgiveness of your sins. And you will receive the gift of the Holy Spirit.'"*

Baptism marks a change of allegiance. Before baptism, we live under the world's rule—dominated by sin, self, and spiritual darkness. But in baptism, we declare that Jesus is King over our lives, and we step into a new way of living under His reign.

Living as Citizens of God's Kingdom

Once we enter the Kingdom through baptism, we must live as Kingdom citizens. This means aligning our lives with Jesus' teachings and embracing the values of His rule.

1. A New Way of Thinking

The Kingdom of God operates on different principles than the world. Jesus taught a radical way of living—one that values humility, love, and service over power and selfishness.

- **Matthew 5:3-10** – The Beatitudes show the values of God's Kingdom—humility, mercy, peacemaking, and righteousness.

- **Romans 12:2** – *"Do not conform to the pattern of this world, but be transformed by the renewing of your mind."*

2. Obedience to the King

Jesus is not just our Savior—He is our King. To live in His Kingdom means we must obey His commands and follow His way of life.

- **Luke 6:46** – *"Why do you call me, 'Lord, Lord,' and do not do what I say?"*
- **John 14:15** – *"If you love me, keep my commands."*

3. Expanding the Kingdom

The Kingdom of God is meant to grow. We are called to share the good news and invite others to follow Jesus.

- **Matthew 28:19-20** – *"Therefore go and make disciples of all nations, baptizing them in the name of the Father and of the Son and of the Holy Spirit."*

- **Acts 1:8** – *"But you will receive power when the Holy Spirit comes on you; and you will be my witnesses in Jerusalem, and in all Judea and Samaria, and to the ends of the earth."*

Living in the Kingdom is not just about personal salvation—it is about being part of God's mission to bring His rule to the world.

Practical Applications

1. **Daily Surrender to Jesus' Rule** – Begin each day by committing to follow Jesus in your actions and decisions.
2. **Study Jesus' Teachings** – Regularly read the Gospels to understand what it means to live under God's rule.
3. **Seek First the Kingdom** – Prioritize God's mission and values over personal gain (Matthew 6:33).
4. **Share the Good News** – Look for opportunities to tell others about Jesus and invite them into His Kingdom.

Reflection Questions

1. How does understanding the Kingdom of God change your view of baptism?
2. Are there areas in your life where you are still living by the world's values instead of God's Kingdom values?
3. What practical steps can you take to live more fully as a citizen of God's Kingdom?
4. How can you be involved in expanding God's Kingdom by sharing the gospel?

Disciple's Prayer

"Lord Jesus, You are my King. Thank You for rescuing me from the kingdom of darkness and bringing me into Your Kingdom of light. Teach me to live under Your rule, to obey Your commands, and to reflect Your love and truth to the world. Help me seek first Your Kingdom and be faithful in sharing Your gospel. May Your Kingdom come, and Your will be done in my life today and always. Amen."

Baptism is not just about forgiveness—it is about stepping into a new Kingdom where Jesus reigns. As we continue this study, let us embrace our role as Kingdom citizens, living under the authority of Christ and spreading His rule to those around us.

SESSION FIVE:
LIGHT & DARKNESS

Leaving Darkness and Walking in the Light of Christ

Baptism is more than just a symbolic event; it is a spiritual transfer from darkness into light. The Bible teaches that without Christ, we are lost in the kingdom of darkness, enslaved to sin, and separated from God. In baptism, we step into the light of God's truth, forgiveness, and new identity.

In this session, we will explore what it means to leave the darkness behind, walk in the light of Jesus, and live as children of light after baptism.

Key Scriptures

1 John 1:5-7
"This is the message we have heard from him and declare to you: God is light; in him there is no darkness at all. If we claim to have fellowship with him and yet walk in the darkness, we lie and do not live out the truth. But if we walk in the light, as he is in the light, we have fellowship with one another, and the blood of Jesus, his Son, purifies us from all sin."

Acts 26:17-18
"I will rescue you from your own people and from the Gentiles. I am sending you to them to open their eyes and turn them from darkness to light, and from the power of Satan to God, so that they may receive forgiveness of sins and a place among those who are sanctified by faith in me."

Ephesians 5:8-10
"For you were once darkness, but now you are light in the Lord. Live as children of light (for the fruit of the light consists in all goodness, righteousness and truth) and find out what pleases the Lord."

The Reality of Spiritual Darkness

1. The Condition of the World Without Christ

The Bible teaches that apart from Jesus, we are in darkness. Darkness in Scripture represents ignorance, sin, and separation from God.

- **John 3:19-20** – *"This is the verdict: Light has come into the world, but people loved darkness instead of light because their deeds were evil. Everyone who does evil hates the light and will not come into the light for fear that their deeds will be exposed."*

- **Colossians 1:13** – *"For he has rescued us from the dominion of darkness and brought us into the kingdom of the Son he loves."*

Before baptism, we are enslaved to sin, unable to free ourselves. But Jesus provides the way out of this darkness through salvation.

2. Baptism as a Transfer from Darkness to Light

Baptism is the moment we cross over from darkness into light. It is not merely a ritual but a transformation where we become children of God.

- **Romans 6:3-4** – *"Or don't you know that all of us who were baptized into Christ Jesus were baptized into his death? We were therefore buried with him through baptism into death in order that, just as Christ was raised*
- *from the dead through the glory of the Father, we too may live a new life."*

- **1 Peter 2:9** – *"But you are a chosen people, a royal priesthood, a holy nation, God's special possession, that you may declare the praises of him who called you out of darkness into his wonderful light."*

At baptism, our old selves die, and we are raised to a new life in Christ, leaving the darkness behind and stepping into God's marvelous light.

Living in the Light

Once we have entered the light, we must actively walk in it. This means living in obedience to Christ and reflecting His love and truth.

1. Walking in the Light Means Living Differently

We can no longer live as we once did. Walking in the light requires aligning our lives with God's truth.

- **2 Corinthians 5:17** – *"Therefore, if anyone is in Christ, the new creation has come: The old has gone, the new is here!"*

- **Ephesians 5:8-9** – *"For you were once darkness, but now you are light in the Lord. Live as children of light (for the fruit of the light consists in all goodness, righteousness and truth)."*

2. The Truth Revealed by the Light

Light exposes what is hidden and reveals the truth.

- **John 8:12** – *"When Jesus spoke again to the people, he said, 'I am the light of the world. Whoever follows me will never walk in darkness, but will have the light of life.'"*
- **Psalm 119:105** – *"Your word is a lamp for my feet, a light on my path."*

3. Maintaining Fellowship in the Light

Walking in the light means we have fellowship with God and with other believers.

- **1 John 1:7** – *"But if we walk in the light, as he is in the light, we have fellowship with one another, and the blood of Jesus, his Son, purifies us from all sin."*

- **Hebrews 10:24-25** – *"And let us consider how we may spur one another on toward love and good deeds, not giving up meeting together, as some are in the habit of doing, but encouraging one another."*

Practical Ways to Walk in the Light

1. **Daily Repentance** – Confess sins regularly to stay in the light and maintain a pure heart before God.

2. **Engage in God's Word** – Read and meditate on Scripture to keep your path illuminated.

3. **Stay in Fellowship** – Surround yourself with other believers who encourage you to live in the light.

4. **Live with Integrity** – Let your actions reflect God's truth in every area of life.

5. **Shine for Others** – Be a light to those still in darkness by sharing the love and truth of Jesus.

Reflection Questions

1. What areas of darkness has God called you to leave behind?
2. How does walking in the light change your relationships with others?
3. What steps can you take to stay in the light daily?
4. How can you shine God's light to those around you?

Disciple's Prayer

"Father of Light, thank You for rescuing me from darkness and bringing me into Your marvelous light. Teach me to walk in the light every day, living in truth, love, and righteousness. Help me to reflect Your light to others, so they may see Your goodness and grace. In Jesus' name, Amen."

Baptism is not just about forgiveness—it is about stepping into the light of God's Kingdom. As we continue this study, may we embrace our identity as children of light and shine brightly for Christ in all we do.

SESSION SIX:
NEW TESTAMENT CONVERSION

Understanding Salvation in the Early Church

Baptism is central to the conversion process in the New Testament. Throughout the book of Acts, every instance of someone becoming a Christian includes baptism. It is not just a ritual but a transformative moment where sins are forgiven, the Holy Spirit is received, and one is united with Christ.

This session will explore the biblical pattern of conversion, highlighting how baptism is consistently presented as the moment of salvation and new birth into Christ's Kingdom.

Key Scriptures

Acts 2:38
"Peter replied, 'Repent and be baptized, every one of you, in the name of Jesus Christ for the forgiveness of your sins. And you will receive the gift of the Holy Spirit.'"

Romans 6:3-4
"Or don't you know that all of us who were baptized into Christ Jesus were baptized into his death? We were therefore buried with him through baptism into death in order that, just as Christ was raised from the dead through the glory of the Father, we too may live a new life."

Acts 22:16

"And now what are you waiting for? Get up, be baptized and wash your sins away, calling on his name."

The Pattern of Conversion in Acts

1. Hearing the Gospel Message

Faith begins with hearing the Word of God. The apostles preached about Jesus' death, resurrection, and the necessity of repentance.

- **Romans 10:17** – *"Consequently, faith comes from hearing the message, and the message is heard through the word about Christ."*

- **Acts 8:35** – Philip explained the gospel to the Ethiopian eunuch before his baptism.

2. Believing in Jesus as Lord

A response of faith is necessary before baptism. Believers accept Jesus as Lord and Savior, placing their trust in Him.

- **Acts 16:31** – *"Believe in the Lord Jesus, and you will be saved—you and your household."*

- **John 3:16** – Faith in Jesus is the foundation of salvation.

3. Repenting of Sin

Conversion requires a turning away from sin and a commitment to follow Christ.

- **Acts 2:38** – Peter commanded people to repent and be baptized.

- **Luke 13:3** – Jesus emphasized the need for repentance.

4. Baptism: The Moment of Salvation

In every conversion account in Acts, baptism is immediate, demonstrating its vital role in salvation.

- **Acts 2:41** – *"Those who accepted his message were baptized, and about three thousand were added to their number that day."*
- **Acts 8:36-38** – The Ethiopian eunuch immediately sought baptism.
- **Acts 9:17-18** – Paul (Saul) was baptized after encountering Jesus.
- **Acts 10:47-48** – Cornelius and his household were baptized upon receiving the gospel.
- **Acts 16:14-15, 33** – Lydia and the Philippian jailer were baptized immediately.

5. Receiving the Holy Spirit

The Holy Spirit is given to those who are baptized into Christ.

- **Acts 2:38** – Baptism and the gift of the Holy Spirit are linked.
- **Ephesians 1:13-14** – The Holy Spirit is a seal of salvation.

Examples of Conversion in Acts

- **Acts 2:38** — Pentecost: Repent and be baptized for forgiveness and the gift of the Holy Spirit.

- **Acts 8:12-13** — Samaritans believed and were baptized.

- **Acts 8:36-38** — Ethiopian eunuch was baptized after hearing the gospel.

- **Acts 9:17-18** — Paul was baptized after meeting Jesus.

- **Acts 10:47-48** — Cornelius and his household were baptized.

- **Acts 16:14-15** — Lydia and her household were baptized.

- **Acts 16:30-33** — The Philippian jailer and his household were baptized.

Every conversion included baptism—immediately.

Baptism: A Death, Burial, and Resurrection

Paul explains the significance of baptism in Romans 6. Baptism is not just symbolic; it is a participation in the death, burial, and resurrection of Christ.

- **Romans 6:3-4** – Baptism is a burial with Christ and a resurrection to a new life.

- **Colossians 2:12** – *"Having been buried with him in baptism, in which you were also raised with him through your faith in the working of God, who raised him from the dead."*

Baptism is the point where a believer dies to sin, is buried in water, and rises to live a new life in Christ.

Common Misconceptions About Baptism

1. Is Baptism Just a Symbol?

Some argue that baptism is only an outward sign of an inward faith. However, Scripture teaches that baptism is the moment when sins are forgiven and one is saved.

- **1 Peter 3:21** – *"And this water symbolizes baptism that now saves you also—not the removal of dirt from the body but the pledge of a clear conscience toward God."*

2. Do We Need to Be Baptized to Be Saved?

Jesus Himself commanded baptism (Matthew 28:19), and every conversion in Acts includes it. The New Testament does not separate baptism from salvation.

3. What About the Thief on the Cross?

Some point to the thief on the cross as an example of salvation without baptism. However, this was before Jesus' death and resurrection, meaning baptism in His name had not yet been instituted.

Practical Applications

1. **Understand the Biblical Pattern** – Study the examples in Acts to see how people responded to the gospel.

2. **Evaluate Your Own Baptism** – Have you followed the biblical pattern of conversion?

3. **Teach Others** – Share the truth of baptism with those who may not understand its significance.

4. **Live in Your Baptism** – Recognize that baptism is the start of a transformed life in Christ, walking in righteousness and the power of the Holy Spirit.

Reflection Questions

1. How does the New Testament pattern of conversion compare with your own experience?
2. Why do you think baptism is emphasized so consistently in Scripture?
3. How would you explain the role of baptism to someone new to the faith?
4. What steps can you take to ensure you are living out the commitment you made in baptism?

Disciple's Prayer

"Father, thank You for giving us a clear path to salvation in Your Word. Help me to follow Your plan, not my own ideas. Thank You for the gift of baptism, where my sins were washed away, and I was united with Christ. Let me walk daily in the new life You have given me, and give me the courage to share this truth with others. In Jesus' name, Amen."

Baptism is not optional or merely symbolic; it is an essential part of entering into Christ's salvation. As we continue this study, let us embrace the full depth of God's plan and live as transformed disciples of Jesus Christ.

SESSION SEVEN:
THE CROSS

Understanding the Power and Purpose of the Cross

The cross is the central event in human history—the moment where Jesus took on the sin of the world to bring us salvation. Without the cross, there is no forgiveness, no reconciliation with God, and no hope of eternal life. Understanding the meaning of Jesus' crucifixion is essential for every believer, especially when preparing for baptism. Baptism is not just a ritual; it is our participation in the death, burial, and resurrection of Jesus.

Through baptism, we are not simply participating in a ceremony—we are spiritually united with Jesus in His death, burial, and resurrection. This powerful connection to the cross transforms our identity, breaks the power of sin, and gives us new life.

In this session, we will explore why Jesus had to die, what was accomplished through His sacrifice, and how baptism connects us to the cross.

Key Scriptures

Isaiah 53:5
"But he was pierced for our transgressions, he was crushed for our iniquities; the punishment that brought us peace was on him, and by his wounds we are healed."

Romans 5:8
"But God demonstrates his own love for us in this: While we were still sinners, Christ died for us."

1 Peter 2:24
"He himself bore our sins in his body on the cross, so that we might die to sins and live for righteousness; by his wounds you have been healed."

Why Did Jesus Have to Die?

1. The Problem of Sin

Sin separates us from God. The penalty for sin is death, both physical and spiritual.

- **Romans 3:23** – *"For all have sinned and fall short of the glory of God."*

- **Romans 6:23** – *"For the wages of sin is death, but the gift of God is eternal life in Christ Jesus our Lord."*

Because of our sin, we were under God's judgment and unable to save ourselves.

2. Jesus as the Perfect Sacrifice

The Old Testament system of animal sacrifices temporarily covered sin, but it could not remove it completely. Jesus became the final and perfect sacrifice, fulfilling the requirements of God's justice.

- **Hebrews 10:10** – *"We have been made holy through the sacrifice of the body of Jesus Christ once for all."*

- **John 1:29** – *"Look, the Lamb of God, who takes away the sin of the world!"*

Jesus' death on the cross was not just an act of suffering—it was the divine plan of salvation, demonstrating God's love and justice.

3. A Ransom for Many

Jesus willingly laid down His life to redeem us from sin and death.

- **Mark 10:45** – *"For even the Son of Man did not come to be served, but to serve, and to give his life as a ransom for many."*

- **Galatians 3:13** – *"Christ redeemed us from the curse of the law by becoming a curse for us."*

Through the cross, Jesus paid the price we could never pay, making reconciliation with God possible.

The Power of the Cross

The cross is not just an event of the past—it has ongoing power in our lives today.

1. Forgiveness of Sins

Through Jesus' blood, we receive complete forgiveness.

- **Ephesians 1:7** – *"In him we have redemption through his blood, the forgiveness of sins, in accordance with the riches of God's grace."*

- **Colossians 2:13-14** – *"He forgave us all our sins, having canceled the charge of our legal indebtedness."*

2. Victory Over Death

The cross was not the end—Jesus' resurrection proved His victory over sin and death.

- **1 Corinthians 15:55-57** – *"Where, O death, is your victory? Where, O death, is your sting?"*

- **Revelation 1:18** – *"I am the Living One; I was dead, and now look, I am alive for ever and ever!"*

3. Transformation of Life

The cross not only saves us—it changes us. We are called to live differently because of Christ's sacrifice.

- **2 Corinthians 5:17** – *"If anyone is in Christ, the new creation has come: The old has gone, the new is here!"*

- **Galatians 2:20** – *"I have been crucified with Christ and I no longer live, but Christ lives in me."*

Baptism and the Cross

Baptism is how we personally connect to the power of the cross. It is the moment where we die to sin, are buried with Christ, and rise to a new life.

- **Romans 6:3-4** – *"Don't you know that all of us who were baptized into Christ Jesus were baptized into his death? We were therefore buried with him through baptism into death in order that, just as Christ was raised from the dead through the glory of the Father, we too may live a new life."*

- **Colossians 2:12** – *"Having been buried with him in baptism, in which you were also raised with him through your faith in the working of God, who raised him from the dead."*

Baptism as Spiritual Circumcision

Paul describes baptism as a circumcision of the heart.

- **Colossians 2:11-12** – *"In him you were also circumcised with a circumcision not performed by human hands. Your whole self ruled by the flesh was put off when you were circumcised by Christ, having been buried with him in baptism."*

Just as Old Testament circumcision marked God's covenant people, baptism marks us as belonging to Christ—our old, sinful nature is cut away, and we are made new.

Practical Applications

1. **Embrace the Full Meaning of the Cross** – Reflect on Jesus' sacrifice and what it means for your salvation.

2. **Live in Gratitude** – Worship and thank God daily for the gift of grace through Jesus.

3. **Walk in Newness of Life** – If you have been baptized, live as someone who has died to sin and now walks in the light.

4. **Share the Message of the Cross** – Tell others about Jesus' sacrifice and the salvation He offers.

Reflection Questions

1. How does the cross change your understanding of sin and forgiveness?
2. What does it mean to take up your cross daily and follow Jesus?
3. How does baptism connect you personally to Jesus' death and resurrection?
4. In what ways can you live differently because of Christ's sacrifice?

Disciple's Prayer

"Jesus, thank You for the cross. Thank You for bearing my sins, taking my punishment, and offering me new life. Help me to live in the power of Your resurrection and to never take Your sacrifice for granted. Let my life reflect the grace and love You have given me. In Your name, Amen."

The cross is the foundation of our faith and the source of our salvation. As we continue this study, may we fully grasp the depth of Jesus' sacrifice and commit our lives to Him in response.

SESSION EIGHT:
BAPTISM WITH THE HOLY SPIRIT

Receiving the Gift of God's Presence

Baptism is not just about the forgiveness of sins; it is also about receiving the gift of the Holy Spirit. This promise is at the heart of God's redemptive plan, empowering believers to live holy lives and equipping them for the work of His kingdom. Throughout Scripture, God promised to pour out His Spirit on His people, and in the New Testament, we see the fulfillment of that promise in baptism.

The Holy Spirit is not an impersonal force but the very presence of God dwelling within believers. His role is to guide, convict, strengthen, and transform us into the image of Christ. This session explores how the Holy Spirit works in the life of a believer, the connection between baptism and the Spirit, and the ongoing role of the Spirit in our daily walk with God.

Key Scriptures

Acts 2:38
"Peter replied, 'Repent and be baptized, every one of you, in the name of Jesus Christ for the forgiveness of your sins. And you will receive the gift of the Holy Spirit.'"

John 14:16-17
"And I will ask the Father, and he will give you another advocate to help you and be with you forever—the Spirit of truth. The world cannot accept him, because it neither sees him nor knows him. But you know him, for he lives with you and will be in you."

Romans 8:11
"And if the Spirit of him who raised Jesus from the dead is living in you, he who raised Christ from the dead will also give life to your mortal bodies because of his Spirit who lives in you."

The Holy Spirit at Baptism

1. The Promise of the Holy Spirit

The Holy Spirit was promised as part of God's plan for His people:

- **Ezekiel 36:26-27** – *"I will give you a new heart and put a new spirit in you; I will remove from you your heart of stone and give you a heart of flesh. And I will put my Spirit in you and move you to follow my decrees and be careful to keep my laws."*

- **Joel 2:28-29** – *"And afterward, I will pour out my Spirit on all people. Your sons and daughters will prophesy, your old men will dream dreams, your young men will see visions. Even on my servants, both men and women, I will pour out my Spirit in those days."*

On the Day of Pentecost, Peter connected this Old Testament promise to the New Covenant by proclaiming that the Spirit is given at baptism (Acts 2:38-39). This means every baptized believer receives the Spirit, not just select individuals.

2. The Role of the Holy Spirit in Baptism

Baptism is not just a symbolic act—it is a spiritual rebirth where the Holy Spirit plays an essential role:

- **Titus 3:5** – *"He saved us through the washing of rebirth and renewal by the Holy Spirit."*

- **1 Corinthians 12:13** – *"For we were all baptized by one Spirit so as to form one body—whether Jews or Gentiles, slave or free—and we were all given the one Spirit to drink."*

The Holy Spirit works in baptism to cleanse, renew, and bring believers into the body of Christ. Without the Spirit, baptism would be an empty ritual; with the Spirit, it is a transformative encounter with God.

The Work of the Holy Spirit in a Believer's Life

Once we receive the Holy Spirit, He begins to shape our lives in profound ways. Here are some key aspects of how He works in us:

1. The Holy Spirit Teaches and Reminds Us of God's Word

- **John 14:26** – *"But the Advocate, the Holy Spirit, whom the Father will send in my name, will teach you all things and will remind you of everything I have said to you."*

- **1 Corinthians 2:12** – *"What we have received is not the spirit of the world, but the Spirit who is from God, so that we may understand what God has freely given us."*

2. The Holy Spirit Convicts Us of Sin and Guides Us in Righteousness

- **John 16:8** – *"When he comes, he will prove the world to be in the wrong about sin and righteousness and judgment."*

- **Romans 8:14** – *"For those who are led by the Spirit of God are the children of God."*

3. The Holy Spirit Empowers Us for Mission

- **Acts 1:8** – *"But you will receive power when the Holy*

- *Spirit comes on you; and you will be my witnesses in Jerusalem, and in all Judea and Samaria, and to the ends of the earth."*

- **Ephesians 3:16** – *"I pray that out of his glorious riches he may strengthen you with power through his Spirit in your inner being."*

4. The Holy Spirit Produces Spiritual Fruit in Our Lives

- **Galatians 5:22-23** – *"But the fruit of the Spirit is love, joy, peace, forbearance, kindness, goodness, faithfulness, gentleness and self-control."*

- **2 Corinthians 3:18** – *"And we all, who with unveiled faces contemplate the Lord's glory, are being transformed into his image with ever-increasing glory, which comes from the Lord, who is the Spirit."*

5. The Holy Spirit Intercedes in Prayer

- **Romans 8:26** – *"In the same way, the Spirit helps us in our weakness. We do not know what we ought to pray for, but the Spirit himself intercedes for us through wordless groans."*

When we don't know how to pray, the Holy Spirit prays on our behalf, aligning our hearts with God's will.

Living by the Spirit

Receiving the Spirit at baptism is the beginning of a lifelong relationship with God. Walking by the Spirit means surrendering daily to His guidance and allowing Him to shape our character and actions.

Practical Steps to Walk by the Spirit

1. **Pray for Guidance** – Ask the Holy Spirit to lead you in decisions, relationships, and ministry.

2. **Study God's Word** – The Spirit teaches and reminds us of Scripture. Meditate on the Bible daily.

3. **Listen to Conviction** – When you feel prompted to turn away from sin, respond in obedience.

4. **Rely on God's Strength** – When you feel weak, remember that the Spirit who raised Jesus from the dead lives in you (Romans 8:11).

5. **Live in Community** – Fellowship with other Spirit-filled believers to encourage and strengthen one another.

Reflection Questions

1. How does knowing that the Holy Spirit lives in you change your perspective on your faith journey?

2. In what areas of your life do you need to rely more fully on the Spirit's guidance and power?

3. How can you become more aware of the Spirit's presence in your daily life?

4. How has the Holy Spirit already worked in your life since your baptism?

Disciple's Prayer

"Father, thank You for the gift of Your Spirit, given at my baptism. Help me to walk by Your Spirit every day, relying on His power, listening to His voice, and following His lead. Teach me to depend on You in all things. Fill me with Your Spirit's wisdom, courage, and love. In Jesus' name, Amen."

Baptism with the Holy Spirit is not a one-time event but an ongoing relationship with God's presence in our lives. As we continue this study, may we commit to walking in step with the Spirit, allowing Him to transform us and use us for God's glory.

SESSION NINE:
MIRACULOUS GIFTS OF THE HOLY SPIRIT

Understanding the Spirit's Power and Purpose

The Holy Spirit plays a crucial role in the life of every believer, providing guidance, strength, and transformation. However, the Spirit also grants miraculous gifts to confirm the gospel message and empower the church. These gifts, which include healing, prophecy, speaking in tongues, and other supernatural signs, continue to manifest in the lives of believers today. The same Spirit who worked powerfully in the early church is still active today, equipping God's people to accomplish His will.

In this session, we will explore the nature and purpose of miraculous gifts, how they functioned in the New Testament, and how they continue to operate in the lives of believers today. Understanding these gifts deepens our faith and reminds us that God is still moving powerfully in the world.

Key Scriptures

1 Corinthians 12:4-7
"There are different kinds of gifts, but the same Spirit distributes them. There are different kinds of service, but the same Lord. There are different kinds of working, but in all of them and in everyone it is the same God at work. Now to each one the manifestation of the Spirit is given for the common good."

Hebrews 2:3-4
"This salvation, which was first announced by the Lord, was

confirmed to us by those who heard him. God also testified to it by signs, wonders, and various miracles, and by gifts of the Holy Spirit distributed according to his will."

Mark 16:17-18
"And these signs will accompany those who believe: In my name they will drive out demons; they will speak in new tongues; they will pick up snakes with their hands; and when they drink deadly poison, it will not hurt them at all; they will place their hands on sick people, and they will get well."

The Purpose of Miraculous Gifts

God grants miraculous gifts for specific reasons, and they continue to serve important purposes today:

1. **To Confirm the Gospel Message**

    - **Mark 16:20** – *"Then the disciples went out and preached everywhere, and the Lord worked with them and confirmed his word by the signs that accompanied it."*

    - **Hebrews 2:3-4** – Miracles performed by believers testify to the truth of the gospel.

2. **To Build Up and Strengthen the Church**

    - **Ephesians 4:11-12** – "So Christ himself gave the apostles, the prophets, the evangelists, the pastors and teachers, to equip his people for works of service, so that the body of Christ may be built up."

    - The gifts enable the church to function and grow, empowering believers to fulfill their calling.

3. **To Demonstrate God's Power and Love**

    o **Acts 3:6-8** – Peter healed a lame man at the temple, leading many to believe in Jesus.

    o **Acts 5:12-16** – The apostles performed miraculous healings and signs, and more people came to faith.

    o Miracles today serve as a reminder that God is active and working in our lives.

How Are Miraculous Gifts Given?

1. Through the Holy Spirit's Sovereign Choice

Miraculous gifts are not limited to the apostles but are given as the Holy Spirit determines.

- **1 Corinthians 12:11** – "All these are the work of one and the same Spirit, and he distributes them to each one, just as he determines."
- **Romans 12:6** – "We have different gifts, according to the grace given to each of us."
- The Spirit continues to distribute gifts today, equipping believers for ministry.

2. Through Prayer and Seeking God's Will

- **Luke 11:13** – "If you then, though you are evil, know how to give good gifts to your children, how much more will your Father in heaven give the Holy Spirit to those who ask him!"

- **1 Corinthians 14:1** – "Follow the way of love and eagerly desire gifts of the Spirit, especially prophecy."
- Believers are encouraged to seek the gifts of the Spirit and remain open to His leading.

Different Types of Miraculous Gifts in the New Testament

The Bible describes various supernatural abilities given by the Holy Spirit:

1. **Prophecy** – Speaking words directly from God.

2. **Healing** – Supernatural physical healing through prayer and faith.

3. **Speaking in Tongues** – Speaking in languages not previously learned, both for personal edification and for the church.

4. **Interpretation of Tongues** – Understanding and explaining messages given in tongues.

5. **Words of Knowledge and Wisdom** – Special divine insight and wisdom for guidance and decision-making.

6. **Miraculous Powers** – Acts of divine intervention, such as deliverance from demons or supernatural protection.

Are Miraculous Gifts for Today?

The Bible teaches that **miraculous gifts have not ceased** but continue to be active where the Spirit moves.

1. The Gifts Are Meant to Continue

- **1 Corinthians 13:8-10** – While some believe this passage teaches that gifts would cease, the "completeness" mentioned refers to the return of Christ, not the completion of Scripture.

- Until Jesus returns, the church still needs the power of the Holy Spirit.

2. The Holy Spirit Continues to Move

- **Acts 2:17-18** – "In the last days, God says, I will pour out my Spirit on all people... even on my servants, both men and women, I will pour out my Spirit in those days, and they will prophesy."

- Many testimonies around the world confirm ongoing miracles, healings, and manifestations of the Spirit's power.

3. Scripture Encourages Us to Desire Spiritual Gifts

- **1 Corinthians 14:39** – "Therefore, my brothers and sisters, be eager to prophesy, and do not forbid speaking in tongues."

- Rather than rejecting miraculous gifts, believers are called to seek them with discernment and faith.

How Does the Holy Spirit Work in Us Today?

Even though the way gifts manifest may vary, the Spirit continues to be active in believers' lives:

1. **Empowering for Ministry** – The Spirit gives strength and boldness to share the gospel (Acts 1:8).
2. **Healing and Miracles** – God still heals today through prayer and faith (James 5:14-15).
3. **Prophetic Encouragement** – The Spirit gives insight to strengthen and guide believers (1 Thessalonians 5:19-21).
4. **Interceding in Prayer** – The Spirit prays for us when we don't know how (Romans 8:26).
5. **Transforming Our Lives** – The Spirit produces fruit such as love, joy, and peace (Galatians 5:22-23).

Practical Applications

1. **Be Open to the Holy Spirit** – Ask God to work through you however He chooses.
2. **Seek Spiritual Gifts** – Pray and ask for the gifts God wants to give you (1 Corinthians 14:1).
3. **Use Your Gifts in Love** – All gifts should be used to build up the church (1 Corinthians 13:1-3).
4. **Trust in God's Power** – Expect the Holy Spirit to move in your life and the world.

Reflection Questions

1. How has the Holy Spirit worked in your life through spiritual gifts?
2. Which gifts do you feel God may be calling you to seek or develop?
3. How can you use spiritual gifts to strengthen the church and glorify God?
4. Why is it important to remain open to the Holy Spirit's power today?

Disciple's Prayer

"Father, thank You for the gift of Your Spirit and the power You have given to Your people. I ask that You would fill me with Your Spirit, guide me in understanding my gifts, and use me to build up Your church. Help me to walk in faith, relying on Your power to accomplish Your will. I submit myself to You and trust that You will work through me for Your glory. In Jesus' name, Amen."

SESSION TEN:
THE CHURCH

Becoming Part of God's Family

Baptism is not just an individual commitment—it is also how God brings us into His family, the church. The church is not a building, an event, or a religious institution. It is a living, unified body of believers, connected by faith in Jesus and committed to growing together in love and obedience to Him. Through baptism, we become part of this divine community, where we are called to serve, encourage one another, and advance God's mission.

Understanding the church is essential to living out your faith. It is where you will grow, be strengthened, and walk alongside others who are seeking to follow Jesus. In this session, we will explore what the Bible says about the church, why it is important, and how we are meant to be active members of this body.

Key Scriptures

Acts 2:41-42
"Those who accepted his message were baptized, and about three thousand were added to their number that day. They devoted themselves to the apostles' teaching and to fellowship, to the breaking of bread and to prayer."

1 Corinthians 12:12-13
"Just as a body, though one, has many parts, but all its many parts form one body, so it is with Christ. For we were all baptized by one Spirit so as to form one body—whether Jews or Gentiles, slave or free—and we were all given the one Spirit to drink."

Ephesians 4:15-16
"Instead, speaking the truth in love, we will grow to become in every respect the mature body of him who is the head, that is, Christ. From him the whole body, joined and held together by every supporting ligament, grows and builds itself up in love, as each part does its work."

What is the Church?

The word **church** comes from the Greek word *ekklesia*, which means "called out assembly." The church is not just a social group or a religious gathering—it is a people set apart by God for His purposes.

1. The Church is the Body of Christ

- **1 Corinthians 12:27** – "Now you are the body of Christ, and each one of you is a part of it."
- Just as a body has different parts that function together, the church consists of diverse individuals who serve different roles but work as one in Christ.

2. The Church is the Family of God

- **Ephesians 2:19** – "Consequently, you are no longer foreigners and strangers, but fellow citizens with God's people and also members of his household."
- In Christ, we are not alone—we are adopted into God's family, where we belong and grow together.

3. The Church is God's Temple

- **1 Peter 2:5** – "You also, like living stones, are being built into a spiritual house to be a holy priesthood."

- The church is a spiritual dwelling where God's presence is made known and worshipped.

What Happens When You Are Baptized into the Church?

When we are baptized, we are added to God's church and begin a new life of faith within a community of believers. The early church in Acts 2 provides a clear example of what being part of the church looks like.

1. **We Are Added to the Body**

    - **Acts 2:41** – "Those who accepted his message were baptized, and about three thousand were added to their number that day."
    - Baptism is the entrance into the church—the family of God.

2. **We Devote Ourselves to Growth**

    - **Acts 2:42** – "They devoted themselves to the apostles' teaching and to fellowship, to the breaking of bread and to prayer."
    - The church is where we learn God's Word, pray, and grow in faith together.

3. **We Build Relationships with Other Believers**

    - **Hebrews 10:24-25** – "And let us consider how we may spur one another on toward love and good deeds, not giving up meeting together."
    - Christianity is not meant to be lived alone. We need encouragement, accountability, and love from others.

4. **We Serve One Another**

    - **Galatians 6:10** – "Therefore, as we have opportunity, let us do good to all people, especially to those who belong to the family of believers."
    - God calls us to use our gifts to serve and bless others.

5. **We Participate in God's Mission**

    - **Matthew 28:19-20** – "Therefore go and make disciples of all nations, baptizing them in the name of the Father and of the Son and of the Holy Spirit, and teaching them to obey everything I have commanded you."
    - The church is God's instrument for spreading the gospel and making disciples.

Practical Ways to Be Active in the Church

1. **Commit to a Local Church** – Find a community of believers where you can grow and serve.

2. **Be Regular in Worship and Fellowship** – Participate in church gatherings and small groups.

3. **Serve with Your Gifts** – Use your God-given talents to build up the body of Christ.

4. **Encourage and Support Others** – Be a source of love and encouragement to fellow believers.

5. **Stay Rooted in the Word** – Continue growing in your faith through Bible study and prayer.

Reflection Questions

1. How does knowing that the church is God's family change the way you see your role as a believer?

2. In what ways can you actively participate in the life of your church?

3. How can you use your gifts to serve and encourage others in the church?

4. Why is it important to stay connected to a local church?
5. How does being part of the church strengthen your faith?

Disciple's Prayer

"Father, thank You for bringing me into Your family through baptism. Help me to love and serve my brothers and sisters in Christ. Show me how to use my gifts to build up Your church and bring glory to Your name. Keep me rooted in Your Word and connected to the body of believers so that I may grow and encourage others in faith. In Jesus' name, Amen."

SESSION ELEVEN:
OVERVIEW OF THE BOOK OF ACT

The Birth and Growth of the Church

The Book of Acts is a powerful historical account of how the early church began, how the Holy Spirit moved among believers, and how the gospel spread from Jerusalem to the ends of the earth. It bridges the gap between the ministry of Jesus and the establishment of His church, showing us the importance of baptism, discipleship, and living in the power of the Holy Spirit.

Understanding the Book of Acts helps us see how God continues to work in His people today. The same Spirit that empowered the early disciples is still active, calling us to live boldly in faith and share the message of Jesus.

Key Scriptures

Acts 2:38-39
"Peter replied, 'Repent and be baptized, every one of you, in the name of Jesus Christ for the forgiveness of your sins. And you will receive the gift of the Holy Spirit. The promise is for you and your children and for all who are far off—for all whom the Lord our God will call.'"

Acts 22:16
"And now what are you waiting for? Get up, be baptized and wash your sins away, calling on his name."

Acts 1:8
"But you will receive power when the Holy Spirit comes on you; and you will be my witnesses in Jerusalem, and in all Judea and Samaria, and to the ends of the earth."

Acts 4:12
"Salvation is found in no one else, for there is no other name under heaven given to mankind by which we must be saved."

Acts 9:15
"But the Lord said to Ananias, 'Go! This man is my chosen instrument to proclaim my name to the Gentiles and their kings and to the people of Israel.'"

Major Themes in Acts

1. The Power of the Holy Spirit

- **Acts 2:1-4** – The Holy Spirit is poured out at Pentecost, empowering the disciples to preach boldly.

- **Acts 4:31** – Believers prayed, and the Holy Spirit filled them, giving them courage to proclaim God's word.

- The Spirit is the driving force behind the growth of the church, working through miracles, guidance, and conviction.

2. The Spread of the Gospel

- **Acts 8:4** – "Those who had been scattered preached the word wherever they went."

- The gospel spread from Jerusalem to Judea, Samaria, and the Gentile world, fulfilling Jesus' command in Acts 1:8.

- The apostles, particularly Peter and Paul, played key roles in taking the gospel to new regions.

3. Baptism and Salvation

- **Acts 2:41** – About 3,000 people were baptized on the day of Pentecost.

- **Acts 8:36-38** – The Ethiopian eunuch was baptized after hearing the gospel.

- Every conversion account in Acts includes baptism, showing its importance in becoming a disciple of Jesus.

4. The Persecution of the Church

- **Acts 5:40-41** – The apostles rejoiced after being flogged for preaching Jesus.

- **Acts 7:59-60** – Stephen became the first Christian martyr.

- Persecution led to the gospel spreading even further as believers fled to new regions.

5. The Role of Paul in Expanding the Church

- **Acts 9:3-6** – Paul encounters Jesus on the road to Damascus and is transformed.

- **Acts 13-28** – Paul embarks on missionary journeys, planting churches and spreading the gospel across the Roman Empire.

- Paul's writings and teachings became foundational for Christian doctrine.

The Acts Conversion Accounts

The Book of Acts provides clear examples of how people became Christians in the early church. Every account follows a pattern of **hearing the gospel, believing in Jesus, repenting of sin, being baptized, and receiving the Holy Spirit.**

1. **The Jews at Pentecost (Acts 2:38-41)** – Peter preaches, and 3,000 are baptized.

2. **The Samaritans (Acts 8:12-17)** – Philip preaches, they believe and are baptized.

3. **The Ethiopian Eunuch (Acts 8:26-39)** – He hears the gospel, believes, and is baptized immediately.

4. **Saul (Paul) (Acts 9:17-18)** – After meeting Jesus, Paul is baptized and receives the Holy Spirit.

5. **Cornelius (Acts 10:47-48)** – The first Gentile believers are baptized.

6. **Lydia (Acts 16:14-15)** – A wealthy woman is baptized along with her household.

7. **The Philippian Jailer (Acts 16:30-33)** – After witnessing a miracle, he and his family are baptized the same night.

Every example shows that **baptism was immediate**, emphasizing its importance in salvation.

What Can We Learn from Acts Today?

The Book of Acts is more than history—it is a blueprint for how we should live as followers of Jesus.

1. Live Boldly Through the Power of the Spirit

- The early disciples faced opposition, but they did not compromise their faith.
- **How can you rely on the Holy Spirit in your daily life?**

2. Share the Gospel Everywhere

- Every believer is called to share their faith, not just preachers and missionaries.
- **Who in your life needs to hear the message of Jesus?**

3. Understand the Role of Baptism

- Baptism is not optional; it is the biblical response to faith in Jesus.
- **Have you been baptized according to the teachings of Acts?**

4. Be Ready to Face Opposition

- The gospel will always face resistance, but God gives us strength to endure.
- **How can you stay strong in your faith when faced with challenges?**

Reflection Questions

1. What stands out to you about the early church in Acts?

2. How does the Book of Acts shape your understanding of the Holy Spirit's work?
3. Why was baptism emphasized in every conversion story in Acts?
4. What lessons from Acts can you apply to your life today?
5. How can you be more active in sharing the gospel like the early believers?

Disciple's Prayer

"Father, thank You for the example of the early church in the Book of Acts. Fill me with Your Spirit, give me boldness to share the gospel, and help me to live in obedience to Your Word. Teach me to follow the example of the first disciples, to endure challenges, and to remain faithful in spreading Your truth. May my life reflect the power of Your Spirit and the message of Jesus. In His name, Amen."

SESSION TWELVE:
AFTER BAPTISM, NOW WHAT

Embracing Your New Life in Christ

Baptism is not the end of the journey—it's the beginning of a new life in Christ. Through baptism, you have been united with Jesus in His death, burial, and resurrection. Now, the call is to walk in this new life, growing in faith, deepening your relationship with God, and living out your faith daily. This session will guide you in understanding what comes after baptism and how to faithfully live as a disciple of Jesus.

Key Scriptures

Romans 6:4
"We were therefore buried with him through baptism into death in order that, just as Christ was raised from the dead through the glory of the Father, we too may live a new life."

Acts 2:42
"They devoted themselves to the apostles' teaching and to fellowship, to the breaking of bread and to prayer."

John 15:5
"I am the vine; you are the branches. If you remain in me and I in you, you will bear much fruit; apart from me you can do nothing."

Hebrews 12:1-2
"Therefore, since we are surrounded by such a great cloud of witnesses, let us throw off everything that hinders and the sin that

so easily entangles. And let us run with perseverance the race marked out for us, fixing our eyes on Jesus, the pioneer and perfecter of faith."

Philippians 4:4-7
"Rejoice in the Lord always. I will say it again: Rejoice! Let your gentleness be evident to all. The Lord is near. Do not be anxious about anything, but in every situation, by prayer and petition, with thanksgiving, present your requests to God. And the peace of God, which transcends all understanding, will guard your hearts and your minds in Christ Jesus."

John 14:15
"If you love me, keep my commands."

The Call to Obedience

After baptism, obedience to Christ is a key part of your faith journey. Jesus calls His followers to not only believe but to put their faith into action by obeying His teachings.

- **Obedience is an Expression of Love**

    - *John 14:15* – "If you love me, keep my commands."
    - Our obedience is not about legalism but about demonstrating our love for Christ through action.

- **Obedience Leads to Spiritual Growth**

    - *James 1:22* – "Do not merely listen to the word, and so deceive yourselves. Do what it says."
    - Following Christ's teachings allows us to mature in faith and be transformed by His Word.

- **Obedience Brings Blessings**
    - *Luke 11:28* – "Blessed rather are those who hear the word of God and obey it."
    - Walking in obedience to God brings peace, joy, and purpose.

Living a New Life

Baptism represents a transformation—dying to sin and rising to a new life in Christ.

- **Dying to Self:** Baptism symbolizes leaving behind the old life of sin.

- **Rising with Christ:** Just as Jesus was resurrected, we are raised to live for Him.

- **Walking in Righteousness:** We are now called to live differently, following God's ways.

Devotion to Spiritual Growth

The early church gives us a model of how to grow in faith after baptism (Acts 2:42). Their devotion to four key practices provides a foundation for every disciple:

1. **The Apostles' Teaching:** Commit to reading and studying Scripture regularly.

2. **Fellowship:** Surround yourself with other believers for encouragement and accountability.

3. **Breaking of Bread:** Participate in communion and reflect on Christ's sacrifice.

4. **Prayer:** Develop a strong prayer life and relationship with God.

Staying Connected to the Vine

Jesus used the analogy of a vine and branches to illustrate how essential it is to remain connected to Him (John 15:5).

- **Stay in the Word:** The Bible is our guide for life.
- **Rely on the Spirit:** The Holy Spirit empowers us to follow Christ.
- **Bear Spiritual Fruit:** Love, joy, peace, and patience will be evident as we grow in Christ.

Running the Race with Perseverance

The Christian life is compared to a race (Hebrews 12:1-2). Baptism is just the starting point—we must continue to run with perseverance.

- **Lay Aside Sin:** Remove distractions that hinder your walk with Christ.
- **Focus on Jesus:** Keep your eyes on Him, not on worldly distractions.
- **Rely on Community:** Surround yourself with believers who encourage your faith.

The Power of Rejoicing and Prayer

Philippians 4:4-7 teaches that joy and peace come through a life of prayer and gratitude.

- **Rejoice in All Circumstances:** True joy comes from knowing Christ.

- **Pray Without Ceasing:** Seek God in all situations.

- **Experience God's Peace:** His peace will guard your heart and mind.

Practical Applications

1. **Daily Devotion:** Set aside time each day for Scripture reading and prayer.

2. **Spiritual Community:** Stay committed to a local church for growth and fellowship.

3. **Serve Others:** Use your gifts to bless and encourage others.

4. **Share Your Faith:** Tell others about your journey with Christ.

5. **Remain Teachable:** Seek guidance from mature believers and stay open to learning.

Reflection Questions

1. What changes have you experienced since your baptism?
2. How are you growing in your faith daily?
3. Who are the people encouraging you in your spiritual walk?
4. How can you stay committed to following Jesus through obedience?
5. What specific steps can you take to live out your faith more fully?

Disciple's Prayer

"Lord, thank You for giving me new life through baptism. Help me to stay faithful in following You daily. Strengthen my faith, guide me through Your Word, and teach me to walk in obedience. Surround me with believers who encourage my faith and help me grow. Let my life be a testimony of Your goodness and grace. In Jesus' name, Amen."

SESSION THIRTEEN:
CHRIST IS YOUR LIFE

When you were baptized into Christ, you didn't just accept a belief system—you received a new identity. Christ became the center of your life, your purpose, and your hope. To live as a disciple means that every area of your life—your relationships, decisions, priorities, and actions—is shaped by your identity in Christ.

Understanding what it means to have Christ as your life transforms everything. Your past no longer defines you; your future is secured in Him. This session will explore how baptism unites you with Christ, how to live by faith, and how to reflect Christ's character in your daily life.

Key Scriptures

Colossians 3:3-4
"For you died, and your life is now hidden with Christ in God. When Christ, who is your life, appears, then you also will appear with him in glory."

Galatians 2:20
"I have been crucified with Christ and I no longer live, but Christ lives in me. The life I now live in the body, I live by faith in the Son of God, who loved me and gave himself for me."

Colossians 3:12-14
"Therefore, as God's chosen people, holy and dearly loved, clothe yourselves with compassion, kindness, humility, gentleness, and patience. Bear with each other and forgive one another if any of you has a grievance against someone. Forgive as the Lord forgave

you. And over all these virtues put on love, which binds them all together in perfect unity."

What It Means to Have Christ as Your Life

Baptism unites us with Christ in His death and resurrection. Our old self is put to death, and we are given a new life that is completely centered on Him.

1. You Died to Your Old Life

- Your sinful nature, old habits, and worldly identity no longer define you.
- *Colossians 3:3* – "For you died, and your life is now hidden with Christ in God."

2. You Now Live in Christ

- Your worth, purpose, and future are rooted in Him.
- *Galatians 2:20* – "The life I now live in the body, I live by faith in the Son of God."

3. Your Future Is Secure

- Your destiny is tied to Christ's return, where you will share in His glory.
- *Colossians 3:4* – "When Christ, who is your life, appears, then you also will appear with him in glory."

Living by Faith in Christ

When Christ is your life, you are called to walk by faith, trusting in Him daily.

1. Daily Surrender

- Each day, you submit your will to His, seeking His guidance in everything.

2. Faith-Driven Choices

- Your decisions are shaped by Christ's wisdom rather than personal desires or worldly standards.

3. Empowered by Love

- God's love compels you to act in ways that reflect His heart.
- *2 Corinthians 5:7* – "For we live by faith, not by sight."

Putting on the Character of Christ

Since Christ is our life, His character should be evident in our actions and relationships.

Colossians 3:12-14 describes what this looks like:

1. Compassion and Kindness

- Seeing others through Christ's eyes and responding with love.

2. Humility and Gentleness

- Treating others with grace, not pride or harshness.

3. Patience and Forgiveness

- Reflecting the mercy you've received from God.

4. Above All, Love

- Love is the defining mark of a disciple.
- *John 13:35* – "By this everyone will know that you are my disciples, if you love one another."

United in Christ

Baptism not only unites us with Christ but also with His people—the Church. In Christ, every barrier falls away.

Galatians 3:27-29
"For all of you who were baptized into Christ have clothed yourselves with Christ. There is neither Jew nor Gentile, neither slave nor free, nor is there male and female, for you are all one in Christ Jesus."

1. Clothed in Christ

- Your identity is found in Him, not in your background, status, or achievements.

2. Unified in Christ

- Every believer, no matter their story, is your brother or sister in Christ.

3. Heirs with Christ

- You share in the promises and inheritance of God's Kingdom.

Practical Applications

1. **Daily Surrender** – Begin each day by offering your plans, desires, and decisions to Christ.

2. **Cultivate Christlike Character** – Identify areas where you need to grow in compassion, patience, humility, or love.

3. **Live by Faith** – Trust God in both the big and small things, knowing He is your life.

4. **Build Unity** – Embrace fellow believers as family, no matter their background.

5. **Reflect Christ in Relationships** – Treat others as Christ treats you—with grace, kindness, and forgiveness.

Reflection Questions

1. In what areas of your life do you need to fully surrender to Christ?
2. How does knowing your life is hidden in Christ affect your sense of purpose and identity?
3. How can you reflect the character of Christ in your relationships—at home, work, or church?
4. What does it mean for you to live by faith, trusting Christ in every area of life?

Disciple's Prayer

"Lord Jesus, thank You for giving me a new life—a life hidden in You. Teach me to live each day surrendered to Your will, trusting Your wisdom, and reflecting Your love. Shape my character to look more like Yours—full of compassion, kindness, humility, patience,

and forgiveness. Help me to live in unity with my brothers and sisters, showing the world that You are my life. In Your name, Amen."

SESSION FOURTEEN: BUILDING STRONG SPIRITUAL RELATIONSHIPS

Christianity is not meant to be lived in isolation. From the very beginning, God designed us for relationships—both with Him and with others. In baptism, we are not only united with Christ, but we also become part of a spiritual family, the Church. Our relationships with fellow believers are meant to encourage, strengthen, and help us grow in faith.

Building strong spiritual relationships is essential for a thriving Christian life. These relationships provide support, accountability, and encouragement as we pursue God together. This session will explore the biblical foundation for Christian relationships, the importance of spiritual friendships, and how we can cultivate meaningful connections that help us stay faithful to God.

Key Scriptures

Ecclesiastes 4:9-10
"Two are better than one, because they have a good return for their labor: If either of them falls down, one can help the other up. But pity anyone who falls and has no one to help them up."

Proverbs 27:17
"As iron sharpens iron, so one person sharpens another."

Hebrews 10:24-25
"And let us consider how we may spur one another on toward love

and good deeds, not giving up meeting together, as some are in the habit of doing, but encouraging one another—and all the more as you see the Day approaching."

John 13:34-35
"A new command I give you: Love one another. As I have loved you, so you must love one another. By this everyone will know that you are my disciples, if you love one another."

Colossians 3:12-14
"Therefore, as God's chosen people, holy and dearly loved, clothe yourselves with compassion, kindness, humility, gentleness and patience. Bear with each other and forgive one another if any of you has a grievance against someone. Forgive as the Lord forgave you. And over all these virtues put on love, which binds them all together in perfect unity."

The Call to Spiritual Unity

In Christ, we are not only forgiven and made new, but we are also adopted into God's family. This spiritual family—the Church—is meant to be a place of love, growth, and encouragement.

1. **Chosen and Loved**
   - *Colossians 3:12* reminds us that we are chosen by God and dearly loved, which forms the basis for how we treat others.

2. **Clothed in Christ-like Character**
   - Compassion, kindness, humility, gentleness, patience, and forgiveness should mark every relationship in the Church.

3. **Bound by Love**
   - Above all, love holds the spiritual family together and unites us in Christ.

The Power of Encouragement and Accountability

The writer of Hebrews urges believers not to neglect meeting together but instead to actively spur one another on toward love and good works.

1. **Regular Fellowship Matters**
   - Consistent gathering with other believers fuels spiritual growth.

2. **Encouragement Strengthens Faith**
   - When we speak truth, celebrate victories, and walk through struggles together, our faith grows deeper.

3. **Accountability Protects Integrity**
   - Trusted spiritual relationships help us stay on the right path, gently correcting and guiding us when needed.

Love as the Mark of Discipleship

Jesus gave a new commandment: to love one another just as He has loved us. This sacrificial, servant-hearted love is the defining mark of true discipleship.

1. **Love Reflects God's Heart**
   - How we treat each other reveals to the world what God is like.

2. **Love is Active**
   - True love isn't just words—it's shown through our actions, sacrifices, and willingness to walk with others in both joy and hardship.

3. **Love Testifies**
    - When the Church loves well, it becomes a witness to the world that God's love is real.

Relationships That Help You Grow

Strong spiritual relationships don't happen by accident—they are intentionally built and nurtured. God calls us to seek out relationships that sharpen our faith and to become the kind of brother or sister who strengthens others.

1. **Spiritual Mentors**
    - Seek out mature believers who can teach and guide you.

2. **Accountability Partners**
    - Develop relationships where you can be honest about your struggles and receive encouragement.

3. **Spiritual Friendships**
    - Surround yourself with fellow disciples who are equally committed to following Jesus.

Practical Ways to Build Strong Spiritual Relationships

1. **Be Intentional About Fellowship**
    - Regularly meet with other believers for encouragement and growth.
    - Join a Bible study group or a discipleship community.

2. **Prioritize Prayer Together**
    - Pray with and for your friends regularly.
        - Keep a prayer journal to track answered prayers and encourage one another.

3. **Serve One Another**
   - Look for ways to serve and help each other in times of need.
   - Acts of kindness strengthen bonds and reflect Christ's love.

4. **Share Your Faith Journey**
   - Be open about your struggles and victories in faith.
   - Encourage each other through personal testimonies and biblical truths.

5. **Handle Conflicts with Grace**
   - Address disagreements with humility and a spirit of reconciliation.
   - Follow *Matthew 18:15-17* to resolve conflicts biblically.

Reflection Questions

1. Who are the people in your life that help strengthen your faith? How can you deepen those relationships?
2. Are there any relationships that need reconciliation or forgiveness? What steps can you take to restore them?
3. How can you be more intentional about encouraging and supporting other believers?
4. In what ways can you serve and build up your spiritual community?

Disciple's Prayer

"Heavenly Father, thank You for the gift of relationships and community. Help me to build strong spiritual connections that encourage and strengthen my faith. Teach me to love as You love, to forgive as You forgive, and to support others in their walk with

You. May my relationships reflect Your grace, truth, and unity. In Jesus' name, Amen."

Building strong spiritual relationships is essential to growing as a disciple of Christ. As we invest in godly friendships, we strengthen our faith, encourage one another, and reflect God's love to the world.

SESSION FIFTEEN:
THE MISSION

Called to a Life of Purpose

The Christian life is more than just personal faith—it is a calling to join in God's mission. Jesus commissioned His disciples to spread the gospel, make disciples, and expand God's Kingdom on earth. This mission is not reserved for a select few but is entrusted to every believer. As followers of Christ, we are called to be His ambassadors, carrying His message of hope, love, and salvation to the world.

Understanding and embracing this mission transforms our perspective on life. We no longer live for ourselves but for God's purposes. This session will explore what it means to live on mission, how to share our faith effectively, and how to align our daily lives with the Great Commission.

Key Scriptures

Matthew 28:19-20
"Therefore go and make disciples of all nations, baptizing them in the name of the Father and of the Son and of the Holy Spirit, and teaching them to obey everything I have commanded you. And surely I am with you always, to the very end of the age."

Acts 1:8
"But you will receive power when the Holy Spirit comes on you; and you will be my witnesses in Jerusalem, and in all Judea and Samaria, and to the ends of the earth."

2 Corinthians 5:20
"We are therefore Christ's ambassadors, as though God were making His appeal through us. We implore you on Christ's behalf: Be reconciled to God."

Romans 10:14-15
"How, then, can they call on the one they have not believed in? And how can they believe in the one of whom they have not heard? And how can they hear without someone preaching to them? And how can anyone preach unless they are sent? As it is written: 'How beautiful are the feet of those who bring good news!'"

Acts 20:24
"However, I consider my life worth nothing to me; my only aim is to finish the race and complete the task the Lord Jesus has given me—the task of testifying to the good news of God's grace."

John 15:5
"I am the vine; you are the branches. If you remain in me and I in you, you will bear much fruit; apart from me you can do nothing."

Jesus' Mission: Seeking and Saving the Lost

Jesus made it clear why He came—to seek and save the lost. His mission wasn't just to teach or perform miracles, but to rescue people from sin and bring them into God's Kingdom. As His disciples, we are called to continue that mission.

1. **The Heart of God**
   - God's love compels Him to pursue the lost, and He invites us to join Him in that pursuit.

2. **A Relentless Pursuit**
   - Jesus never gave up on people, whether they were outcasts, sinners, or religious leaders.

3. **A Clear Focus**
   - Jesus knew His purpose, and His every action pointed toward reconciling people to God.

The Great Commission: Our Call to Action

After His resurrection, Jesus gave His disciples a clear command—the Great Commission. This is our mission statement as the Church and as individual disciples.

1. **Make Disciples**
   - This is more than converting people—it's walking alongside them as they learn to follow Jesus.

2. **Baptize in His Name**
   - Baptism marks the beginning of a disciple's journey, publicly identifying with Christ.

3. **Teach Obedience**
   - Discipleship isn't just knowledge—it's living out God's commands.

4. **His Presence with Us**
   - Jesus promises to be with us every step of the way as we live out the mission.

Bearing Fruit: Living Out the Mission

Jesus said that when we abide in Him, we will bear much fruit. This fruit is not just personal spiritual growth, but also the impact we have on others—sharing the Gospel, making disciples, and reflecting Christ's love to the world.

1. **Staying Connected**
   - Daily connection with Christ through prayer, Scripture, and obedience fuels fruitfulness.

2. **Bearing the Fruit of Changed Lives**
   - As we share the Gospel and invest in others, we help others discover new life in Christ.

3. **Fruit That Lasts**
   - True fruit is not temporary—it's lives transformed for eternity.

Your Baptism Connects to Your Mission

Baptism is not just a personal milestone—it's a commissioning. When you were baptized, you didn't just commit to following Jesus for yourself. You were sent out as His ambassador, empowered to carry the message of salvation to the world.

Romans 6:3-4
"Or don't you know that all of us who were baptized into Christ Jesus were baptized into his death? We were therefore buried with him through baptism into death in order that, just as Christ was raised from the dead through the glory of the Father, we too may live a new life."

1. **New Life, New Mission**
   - Your baptism symbolizes dying to your old life and stepping into a new life of purpose—a life on mission.

Practical Ways to Live on Mission

1. **Share the Gospel in Everyday Life**
   - Look for opportunities to talk about Jesus with friends, family, and coworkers.
   - Be prepared to share your testimony and explain why you follow Christ.
   - Use conversations about life, struggles, and hope to introduce the gospel.

2. **Live a Life That Reflects Christ**
   - Demonstrate kindness, humility, and integrity in your interactions.
   - Show love and grace to others, even in difficult situations.

3. **Support Missions and Evangelism**
   - Pray for missionaries and those working to spread the gospel.
   - Consider going on a mission trip or supporting local outreach efforts.

4. **Make Disciples, Not Just Converts**
   - Help new believers grow in their faith through mentorship and discipleship.

Reflection Questions

1. How do you view your role in God's mission? Are you actively sharing the gospel?
2. What fears or obstacles prevent you from speaking about Jesus? How can you overcome them?
3. In what ways can you be more intentional about making disciples?

Disciple's Prayer

"Heavenly Father, thank You for calling me to be part of Your mission. Help me to see every moment as an opportunity to share Your love and truth. Fill me with the boldness and wisdom of the Holy Spirit, and guide my words and actions to reflect Your grace. Use me to make disciples and lead others into a deeper relationship with You. May I always live with urgency and purpose, knowing that my time here is meant to glorify You. In Jesus' name, Amen."

SESSION SIXTEEN:
PERSECUTION

Following Jesus comes with incredible blessings, but it also comes with challenges. Throughout history, Christians have faced persecution for their faith. Jesus Himself warned His disciples that they would experience hardship because of their commitment to Him. Understanding persecution helps us remain steadfast in our faith and trust in God's promises, no matter what we face.

The Bible teaches that persecution is not a sign of failure but a mark of true discipleship. Those who stand firm in their faith will be blessed and strengthened in their walk with Christ. This session will explore the reality of persecution, how believers should respond, and the eternal rewards promised to those who remain faithful.

Key Scriptures

2 Timothy 3:12
"In fact, everyone who wants to live a godly life in Christ Jesus will be persecuted."

Matthew 5:10-12
"Blessed are those who are persecuted because of righteousness, for theirs is the kingdom of heaven. Blessed are you when people insult you, persecute you and falsely say all kinds of evil against you because of me. Rejoice and be glad, because great is your reward in heaven, for in the same way they persecuted the prophets who were before you."

1 Peter 4:12-14
"Dear friends, do not be surprised at the fiery ordeal that has

come on you to test you, as though something strange were happening to you. But rejoice inasmuch as you participate in the sufferings of Christ, so that you may be overjoyed when his glory is revealed."

Romans 5:3-5
"Not only so, but we also glory in our sufferings, because we know that suffering produces perseverance; perseverance, character; and character, hope."

The Reality of Persecution

Jesus and the apostles made it clear that persecution is inevitable for those who follow Him. From the early Church to today, believers have faced opposition for their faith.

1. Why Christians Face Persecution

- **We Stand for Truth** – The world resists God's truth because it exposes sin (John 3:19-20).

- **Our Allegiance is to Christ** – We serve God, not the world, which can lead to opposition (Matthew 6:24).

- **Spiritual Warfare is Real** – Satan works against those who seek to expand God's Kingdom (Ephesians 6:12).

2. Persecution in the Early Church

- The apostles were beaten, imprisoned, and even killed for preaching the gospel (Acts 5:40-42, Acts 12:1-2).
- Stephen was the first Christian martyr, stoned for boldly proclaiming Christ (Acts 7:54-60).

- Paul endured suffering for the sake of the gospel, facing beatings, imprisonment, and persecution (2 Corinthians 11:23-28).

3. Modern-Day Persecution

- In many parts of the world, Christians still face imprisonment, discrimination, and violence for their faith.
- Even in free societies, believers may be mocked, ridiculed, or ostracized for standing firm in biblical truth.

Responding to Persecution

How should believers respond when they face opposition for their faith? The Bible provides clear guidance on how to endure persecution with faith and courage.

1. Rejoice and Be Glad

- Jesus tells us to rejoice when persecuted because it means we are standing firm in our faith (Matthew 5:12).
- Paul and Silas praised God even while in prison, showing that joy in suffering is possible (Acts 16:25).

2. Trust in God's Strength

- Relying on Christ helps us stand firm under pressure (Philippians 4:13).
- God gives us the endurance we need to remain faithful (2 Timothy 1:7).

3. Pray for Those Who Persecute You

- Jesus commands us to love and pray for our enemies (Matthew 5:44).

- Stephen prayed for those who stoned him, just as Jesus did on the cross (Acts 7:60, Luke 23:34).

4. Remain Faithful to the Mission

- The apostles continued preaching despite opposition (Acts 4:18-20).
- Paul saw persecution as an opportunity to advance the gospel (Philippians 1:12-14).

The Reward for Enduring Persecution

God promises great rewards for those who remain faithful under persecution.

1. **A Heavenly Reward** – Those who endure will receive a crown of life (Revelation 2:10).
2. **Deeper Spiritual Strength** – Suffering refines our faith and draws us closer to God (Romans 5:3-5).
3. **A Powerful Testimony** – Our endurance shows the world the power of Christ (1 Peter 3:15-16).

Practical Ways to Prepare for Persecution

- **Deepen Your Faith** – Spend time in God's Word daily to strengthen your trust in Him.
- **Surround Yourself with a Strong Christian Community** – Fellowship provides support and encouragement.
- **Develop a Prayer Life** – Seek God's guidance and strength in times of trial.
- **Stay Bold in Sharing the Gospel** – Don't let fear silence your witness.

- **Remember God's Promises** – Meditate on scriptures that remind you of His faithfulness.

Reflection Questions

1. Have you ever faced opposition because of your faith? How did you respond?
2. What are some ways you can prepare yourself to stand firm in the face of persecution?
3. How does knowing that persecution brings rewards help you endure challenges?
4. How can you support and encourage other believers who are facing persecution?

Disciple's Prayer

"Heavenly Father, I thank You for the strength You give me to stand firm in my faith. I know that persecution is a reality, but I trust in Your promises. Help me to remain bold, joyful, and steadfast, even in the face of trials. Give me love for my enemies and courage to share Your truth no matter the cost. Strengthen my

faith and remind me that my reward is in heaven. In Jesus' name, Amen."

Persecution is not something to fear but an opportunity to grow stronger in faith and bring glory to God. As we face challenges, let us stand firm, trusting in His power and promises.

Your Life, Your Baptism, Your Calling

You have walked through the foundational truths of baptism, exploring the **heart of God**, the **call to discipleship**, the **power of the cross**, and the **gift of the Holy Spirit**. You've learned what it means to leave **darkness** behind and walk in the **light**, to **embrace the family of God**, and to **join the mission of Christ**.

Baptism was never meant to be the finish line. It is the **beginning** of a transformed life — a life surrendered to the King, empowered by the Spirit, and marked by bold faith, enduring love, and a relentless commitment to God's mission.

You Are a Disciple

You are more than a believer — you are a **disciple**. You are called to seek God with all your heart, to build your life on His Word, and to follow Jesus wherever He leads, no matter the cost. You are no longer defined by your past, your failures, or the opinions of others. You are defined by **Christ in you**, the hope of glory.

You Belong to God's Family

You were not baptized into isolation. You were baptized into a **family**, a body of believers where each member matters and each disciple has a role to play. Stand with your brothers and sisters. Encourage, forgive, challenge, and love one another deeply — because the world will know you belong to Jesus by the **way you love**.

You Are Sent

Jesus didn't just save you — He **sent you**. Your life is now part of the greatest mission in human history: making disciples of all nations. You are called to be **a light in the darkness**, a voice of truth, and a living testimony to the transforming power of God's grace. Whether in your home, your workplace, your neighborhood, or across the world — **you are sent**.

You Will Face Opposition

The road ahead will not always be easy. As you stand for Christ, expect resistance. But take heart — you are never alone. The Spirit of God lives within you, the Word of God strengthens you, and the people of God stand beside you. **Persevere** with courage, knowing that your faithfulness brings glory to God and points others to His truth.

Your Charge

- **Seek God First.** Pursue Him with all your heart, soul, mind, and strength.
- **Live the Word.** Build your life on Scripture and obey God's commands with joy.
- **Embrace the Cross.** Die to self daily and follow Jesus, no matter the cost.
- **Love the Church.** Commit to your spiritual family, walking in unity, forgiveness, and love.
- **Make Disciples.** Share your story, proclaim the Gospel, and help others follow Jesus.
- **Endure with Faith.** Stand firm in trials, trusting God's promises and holding on to hope.
- **Walk by the Spirit.** Let the Holy Spirit guide, empower, and transform you each day.

Final Encouragement

This is the life you were made for — a life fully surrendered to Jesus. The world may not always understand your faith, but heaven celebrates every step you take in obedience. You are **chosen**, **called**, and **sent**. Walk boldly in the new life Christ has given you. Your baptism was only the beginning.

Philippians 1:6

"Being confident of this, that he who began a good work in you will carry it on to completion until the day of Christ Jesus."

Go forward — live the life you were baptized into — and never turn back.

In Jesus' Name. Amen.

About the Author

Shane Wahner is a dedicated teacher, entrepreneur, and author with a passion for guiding others in their faith journey. His life has been shaped by a relentless pursuit of truth, a deep love for the Word of God, and a commitment to helping people grow spiritually and succeed in all aspects of life.

Having explored various religious traditions and philosophies before reaffirming his faith in Jesus, Shane understands the importance of building a strong spiritual foundation. His experiences have led him to develop *Know the Truth: A Foundational Study for Baptism*, a study designed to help seekers and believers understand the core principles of faith, the authenticity of Scripture, and the transformative power of baptism.

Beyond his work in ministry, Shane is an accomplished entrepreneur, speaker, and mentor, known for his leadership in business and his passion for teaching biblical success principles. He has used his platform to inspire others to seek wisdom, apply biblical truths, and live purpose-driven lives.

Shane's teachings emphasize not only the importance of faith but also the practical application of biblical principles in everyday life. Through his books, music, and public speaking, he continues to empower individuals to grow in their relationship with God and fulfill their divine calling.

You can find Shane's music on all major streaming platforms under his name, or visit www.knowthetruthfoundation.com to explore his latest books and music.

Shane Wahner
Author of the *Know The Truth* Series

Made in the USA
Middletown, DE
21 March 2025